Messerschmitt Bf 109
in action

by John R. Beaman, Jr. & Jerry L. Campbell

illustrated by Don Greer

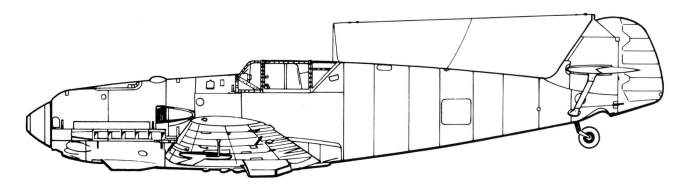

squadron/signal publications

(Cover) *Obstlt*. Adolf Galland and an impromptu wingman return from a *Freijagd* mission over England, Fall 1940.

ISBN 0-89747-106-7

If you have any photographs of the aircraft, armor, soldiers or ships of any nation, particularly wartime snapshots, why not share them with us and help make Squadron/Signal's books all the more interesting and complete in the future. Any photograph sent to us will be copied and the original returned. The donor will be fully credited for any photos used. Please indicate if you wish us not to return the photos. Please send them to: Squadron/Signal Publications, Inc., 1115 Crowley Dr., Carrollton, TX 75011-5010.

Photo Credits

With Thanks To:
Lee Barlow
Bundesarchiv
Hans Obert
IWM
Karl Ries
Smithsonian
Zdenek Titz

Bf 109E-1s of JG 77 immediately prior to the invasion of France. The black boot is the emblem of I *Gruppe*. (Bundesarchiv)

Introduction

It is ironic to think that the Messerschmitt Bf 109, World War II's best known and certainly most numerously produced fighter, was almost discarded out of hand. During the late 1920s, Willy Messerschmitt, at the request of *Deutsche Lufthansa (DLH),* designed a metal, high-wing monoplane airliner capable of carrying ten passengers. Built by *Bayerische Flugzeugwerke (BFW),* Messerschmitt's production sister company, the M-20 airliner prototype crashed on 26 February 1928, the pilot being killed when he tried to jump from 250 feet. The head of *DLH,* Erhard Milch, immediately cancelled the order. In August the second prototype was flown and, when the M-20 was pronounced safe, *DLH* purchased two machines and ordered a further ten. Before deliveries were completed, however, two M-20s crashed in rapid succession. In one of the crashes eight *Reichswehr* officers died with a great deal of publicity appearing in the newspapers and even discussions on the floor of the *Reichstag.* Erhard Milch cancelled all contracts, refused to take delivery of further M-20s, demanded the return of *DLH's* deposits and went so far as to accuse Messerschmitt of "building unsafe aircraft" and being "callous toward the victims of his designs"; both accusations found their way to the newspaper. BFW was thrown into financial ruin and by the end of 1930 registered losses of some 600,000RM. On 1 June 1931 BFW filed bankruptcy proceedings. Messerschmitt Flugzeugbau which had been partially absorbed three years earlier by BFW was able to raise a small amount of additional capital and in cooperation with the BFW receiver managed to force *Lufthansa* to take delivery of the M-20 transports as well as the M-28 high speed mail plane prototype that had originally been ordered. After getting outside financial backing, BFW was reorganized with Willy Messerschmitt at its head.

By the time the Nazis came to power and began their massive rearmament program BFW had begun to recover under the frugal leadership of Messerschmitt. Junkers, Arado, Heinkel, Focke-Wulf, all had aircraft, aircraft that were to be the building blocks of a resurrected, if as yet clandestine, *Luftwaffe.* BFW however received only a contract to manufacture 12 Heinkel He 45 biplanes under license. Erhard Milch, now the Reich Commissioner for Aviation, made it abundantly clear that Messerschmitt would not be receiving contracts to design and build aircraft for the *Luftwaffe,* but would only to build aircraft designed by others under license.

Trying to hold his small design staff together and unable to get design contracts in Germany, Messerschmitt solicited foreign business. A contract was made with I.C.A.R. in Romania for the design of a high wing transport aircraft. Ever eager to embarrass Messerschmitt, Milch's man in charge of the *Luftwaffe* technical office, Oberstleutnant Wilhelm Wimmer, officially rebuked BFW for soliciting foreign business at a "time when the German nation was in great need of aircraft manufacturers". BFW vehemently and

The Kestrel V-powered Bf 109a (D-IABI). A brace was added to the landing gear during initial trials.

loudly pointed out that since they had received no contracts they had no choice but to solicit foreign business. Finally a design contract came forth but under the circumstances it did little to increase Messerschmitt's standing. The progeny of the contract, however, was a different matter. The Bf 108 *Taifun,* a low-wing, all-metal two-seat sport plane, was a remarkably advanced aircraft with excellent flying characteristics. Built for the *Challenge de Tourisme Internationale,* the Bf 108 took fifth, sixth and tenth places.

Early in 1934, even before the Bf 108 made its maiden flight, the *Luftwaffenführungstaab* issued specifications and development contracts for a single engine fighter which would replace the Heinkel He 51, then Germany's first-line fighter, to Arado, Focke-Wulf, Heinkel and reluctantly, after much argument, to BFW. Messerschmitt was semi-officially assured that BFW would receive no production order and was encouraged to refuse the development contract which called for the construction of three prototypes.

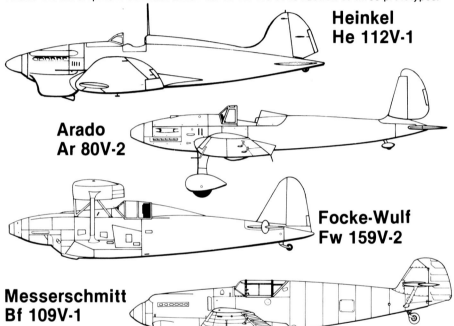

Heinkel He 112V-1

Arado Ar 80V-2

Focke-Wulf Fw 159V-2

Messerschmitt Bf 109V-1

Disregarding the official discouragement, and with little to lose, Messerschmitt decided to build a state-of-the-art aircraft incorporating all the latest technology: a flush-riveted, all-metal, stressed-skin, low-wing cantilever monoplane with slotted flaps on the trailing edge and automatic slots on the leading edge; fully retractable, single-oleo landing gear; fully enclosed cockpit with the narrowest possible fuselage section that would still take the most powerful engine available in Germany — the Junkers Jumo 210, then under development. Provision was made to install the more powerful Daimler Benz DB 600, also under development. Messerschmitt himself led the design team.

Cutting metal for the Bf 109 prototypes was begun in late 1934 and by August of the following year the first prototype, the **Bf 109a** was ready for engine installation when Ernst Udet, then still a private citizen, stopped by the BFW factory. Proudly shown the Bf 109a, Udet after a cursory look exclaimed that: "This machine will never make a fighter"*

Since the anticipated Junkers Jumo 210 powerplant was not yet ready, the RLM instructed BFW to install a Rolls-Royce Kestrel V 12-cylinder engine rated at 695hp at take off, driving a two-bladed Schwarz wooden propeller. In September, carrying the civil registry codes D-IABI and with BFW's chief test pilot, *Flugkapitän* Hans Knötzsch, at the

*Udet would later become an Ardent champion of Messerschmitt's progeny.

The Bf 109V3 (D-IOQV), was the third prototype and mounted three MG 17s, one of which fired through the specially designed cropped spinner. Painted overall RLM Gray, the tail band was red and codes were in black.

controls the Bf 109a made several runs across the field before lifting into the air for the first time. After cranking up the landing gear Knötzsch made several circuits around the field under the watchful eye of Messerschmitt, staying airborne for about twenty minutes. The world's most advanced fighter had flown beautifully — months before the Supermarine Spitfire, which was destined to become its chief antagonist.

After further preliminary factory testing, Knötzsch flew the prototype, now officially designated **Bf 109V-1**, to the *Erprobungsstelle* (Proving Center) at Rechlin. On touching down at Rechlin one of the undercarriage oleos gave way causing minor damage and much satisfaction among Messerschmitt's enemies.

While not necssarily among Messerschmitt's enemies, the test pilots were biased against the Bf 109 with its steep ground angle, automatic wing leading edge slots and high wing loading. The day of the lightly loaded, highly maneuverable biplane was gone but the pilots at Rechlin still retained their bias against the monoplane. On good terms with the *RLM*, the Heinkel design team of Walter and Siegfried Günter was strongly influenced by the opinions of these traditionalists in the Luftwaffe. In an attempt to satisfy the former biplane pilots, the Heinkel fighter was designed around an inordinately large, broad-cord, semi-elliptical wing spanning just over 41 feet. The cockpit was considerably roomier and was open. Willy Messerschmitt, hardly on speaking terms with many of the *RLM* personnel came under no such influence. The He 112 was, as expected, well received at Rechlin by the *E-Stelle* pilots and, even though the officials were obviously impressed with the Bf 109V-1's superior rate of climb, dive and level flight, the Heinkel aircraft was just as obviously the favored aircraft.

Construction of the second and third prototypes had been progressing well and in October 1935 when the Jumo 210A engine became available the second prototype, the **Bf 109V-2 (D-IUDE)** was completed. The V-2, with the exception of the Jumo 210A powerplant providing 610hp at take-off, differed from the V-1 in only minor respects. The undercarriage was strengthened, a gun cooling vent was introduced just behind the top of the spinner and provision was made for the installation of a pair of MG 17s to be mounted over and behind the engine with 500 rpg. In the event, actual gun installation was not accomplished until the third prototype. The Bf 109V-2 began flight trials in January 1936 but, because of powerplant delays, the **Bf 109V-3** did not join the program until June 1936, by which time the *Luftwaffe's* attitude toward Messerschmitt and his advanced fighter had thawed considerably. So much so, in fact, that the *RLM* placed an order for a batch of ten preproduction machines.

In part this thaw came about as a result of German intelligence reports that Supermarine had already received a production order for 310 Spitfires. The rapidity of the order and the close similarity of the Spitfire to the 109 did much to impress the Fighter Acceptance Commission but even more important were the results of flight trials which had dispelled the earlier doubts about the advanced design. The Bf 109 was shown to the

world for the first time when the V-2 was flown over the 11th Olympiad in Berlin in August while the world's first television camera recorded the event.

By November, when definitive evaluation trials were held at Travemünde, the Bf 109 had come full circle, from rank outsider to obvious favorite. With Dr. Ing. Herman Wurster at the controls, the Bf 109 was put through twenty-three left hand spins, immediately followed by twenty-one connsecutive right spins, then a near vertical dive from 23,000 feet. The Heinkel pilot crowned the Bf 109's victory when he decided not to follow. This performance, plus the fact that the Bf 109 was cheaper to build than the Heinkel design, decided the issue. The Bf 109 was chosen as the Luftwaffe's standard first-line fighter.

Just prior to the Travemünde trials the *RLM* issued specifications increasing the fighter's armament from two to three machine guns. A third MG 17 was mounted between the cylinder banks of the Jumo engine, firing through the propeller hub. With a specially designed cropped spinner this was accomplished on the Bf 109V-3.

Each of the preproduction batch were assigned *Versuch* numbers.

Bf 109B-01 — Bf 109V-4
Bf 109B-02 — Bf 109V-5
Bf 109B-03 — Bf 109V-6
Bf 109B-04 — Bf 109V-7
(and so forth)

Flying for the first time in November of 1936 the three-gunned Bf 109V-4 was the last machine to be powered by the Junkers Jumo 210A. The V4 and V5 which joined the test program in December were powered by the improved Jumo 210B offering 600hp for five minutes at sea and a continuous 540hp. Three cooling slots for the guns replaced the single cooling intake and a production windscreen was added.

Since July 1936, civil war had been raging in Spain with the Soviets supporting the Loyalist's side and Germany supporting the Nationalist cause. By November 1936 the *Luftwaffe* had some 4500 "volunteers" of the *Legion Condor* committed to the fighting. Pilots of *Jagdgruppe 88,* the fighter component of the *Legion Condor,* had begun to complain that their Heinkel He 51B biplanes were outclassed in almost every respect by the Russian Polikarpov I-15 fighters. This was viewed with such alarm in Berlin that the three armed prototypes, Bf 109V-3, V4 and V5 were crated up and sent to Spain for service evaluation against the Russian aircraft. After many delays and mechanical breakdowns, none of which were abnormal for such experimental machines, *Jagdgruppe 88* was able to get in enough flying time to prove the marked superiority of the Bf 109 over anything else in the Spanish skies. Oberleutnant Gunther Radusch, who would later become one of the top night-fighter pilots with over 60 kills, got his first victory in the Bf 109:

> We went by ship from Hamburg to Seville disguised as tourists, ten or twelve fighter pilots — our six He 51s were also on board our ship packed in crates. As soon as our aircraft were put together we went into action protecting Ju 52 bombers. At the end of 1936 we got the first Me 109. I got my first victory while flying the Me 109 with only two machine guns. We were flying from Vitorio to protect the bombers, there was a test squadron of bombers (*Kampfgruppe 88: Author's Note*) based north of us. It was a bright day and we had to protect Ju 86s with our three Me 109s. As we approached the harbor I saw four aircraft, Avia 534 biplanes, climbing against the bombers. We caught them just as they came through the bomber formation, we dove and circled behind them. My two companions opened fire too early and three of the Avias peeled away, but the leader didn't seem to notice anything, he stayed quiet. I only had the two machine guns so I closed to fifty meters before I opened fire. When I did, my guns fired a few rounds and quit — it was enough though. The Avia slowly turned over and went down. No smoke, nothing, it fell to about a thousand meters above the ground and then disintegrated.

After nearly three months of intermittant combat duty the prototypes were disassembled and returned to Messerschmitt to continue in the development program.

Bf 109 Development

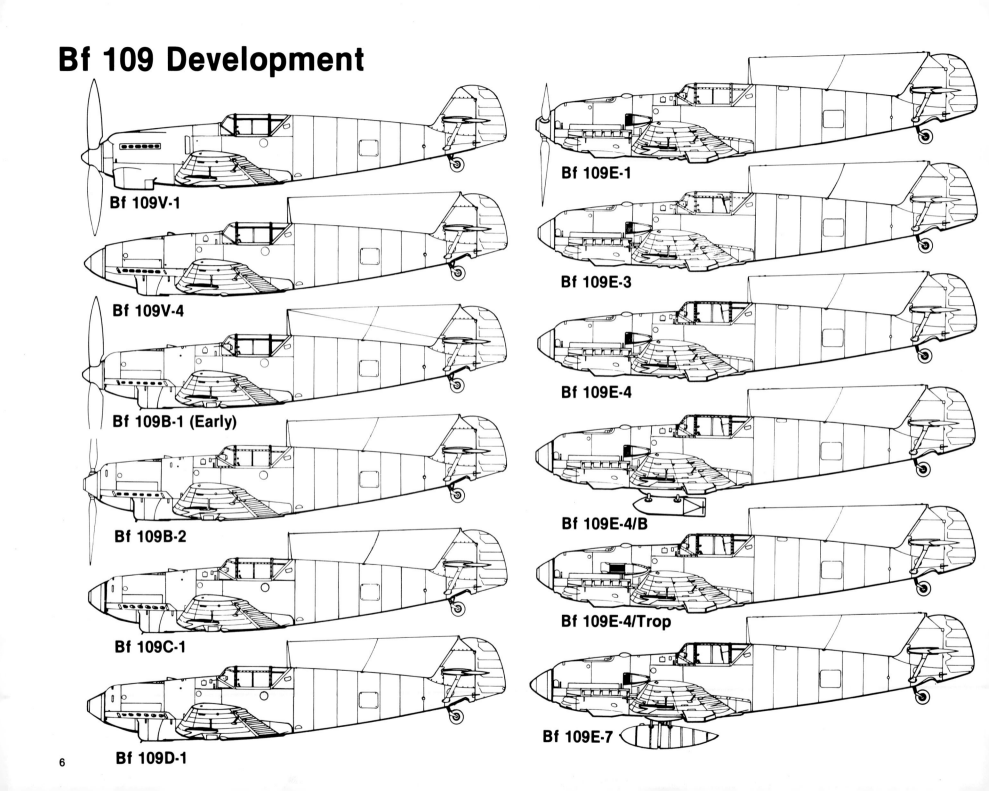

Bf 109V-1

Bf 109V-4

Bf 109B-1 (Early)

Bf 109B-2

Bf 109C-1

Bf 109D-1

Bf 109E-1

Bf 109E-3

Bf 109E-4

Bf 109E-4/B

Bf 109E-4/Trop

Bf 109E-7

Bf 109B-1

Tooling at Augsburg-Haunstetten for the initial production model, the **Bf 109B-1** followed closely behind the batch of ten preproduction B-0 machines, with the first aircraft being delivered in February 1937. They were powered by the improved Jumo 210Da engine with a two-speed supercharger driving a wooden Schwarz fixed-pitch prop and offering 720 h.p. at 2700 r.p.m. for take-off. A Carl Zeiss *Reflexvisier (Revi)* C/12C reflector gun sight was provided. Armament was to have been the three MG 17 configuration but trials in Spain with the V4 found that the engine mounted MG 17 firing through the propeller hub was prone to jamming after a few rounds were fired, due to inadequate cooling, consequently the B-1 was delivered without this gun. The oil cooler was removed from the radiator bath and a separate intake was provided beneath the port wing.

JG 132 *Richthofen* was the first *Jagdgeschwader* scheduled to receive the new fighter as well as being charged with working up a set of suitable fighter tactics. II *Gruppe* at Juterborg-Damm was to convert first with I *Gruppe* at Döberitz converting next. However, due to the increased presence of Russian supplied Polikarpov I-15s and the introduction of the even better I-16 *Rata*, personnel of II/JG 132 were put through a hurried conversion course and immediately posted to Spain, with their Bf 109B-1s, arriving in April 1937. Thus 2./J.88 of the *Legion Condor* became the first operational unit to actually be equipped with the Luftwaffe's premier new Bf 109B-1, relinquishing their He 51s to Spanish forces.

Late B-1

Several minor running changes were made to the B-1 while on the assembly line. The three wire R/T antenna was changed back to a single wire, the three gun-cooling slots introduced on the V5 and V6 were added, as was a small air vent on the port side of the MG 17 access panel immediately in front of the windscreen, which was also lengthened.

The Initial B-1s carried a three wire radio antenna clearly seen on this early B-1, this was quickly changed to a single wire configuration.

Windscreen Development

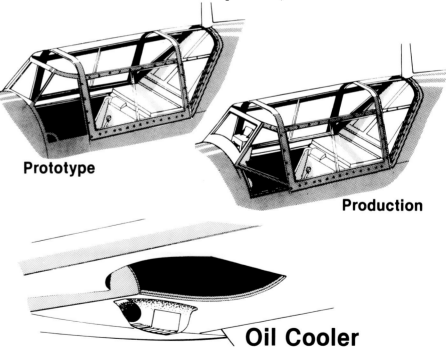

Prototype

Production

Oil Cooler

This early production B-1, as evidenced by the lack of gun cooling slots, was equipped with a fixed pitch Schwarz wooden propeller.

Bf 109B-1 (Late)

This *Legion Condor* late-production B-1 is without a radio as were most machines sent to Spain. Germany's *Legion Condor* was able to battle-test equipment, train personnel and work up fighter tactics while the rest of the world watched and wrung its hands. The Soviet Union, having the same opportunity, lost it when most of the experienced returning 'volunteers' were shot because of their foreign 'taint'.

Cowling Development

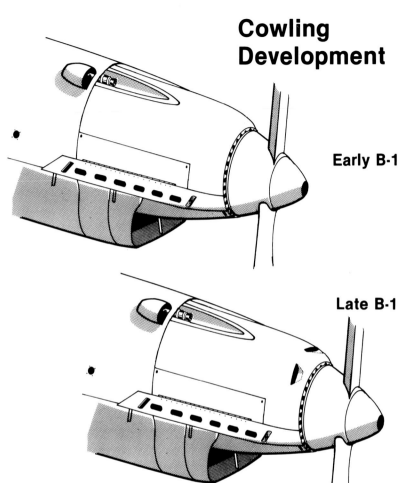

Early B-1

Late B-1

Antenna Development

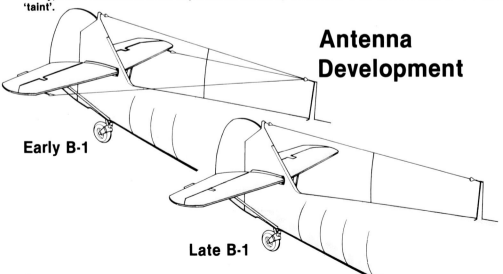

Early B-1

Late B-1

Windscreen Development

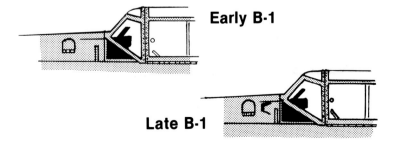

Early B-1

Late B-1

Bf 109B-2

During the summer of 1937, after less than thirty examples of the B-1 were produced, it was replaced on the assembly line by the **Bf 109B-2**, the initial examples of which differed solely in having the fixed-pitch wooden propeller replaced by a variable-pitch, two-bladed prop. Again the first fighters to roll off the assembly line were rushed to Spain, with a total of 40 Bf 109B-1s and B-2s being eventually shipped to the *Legion Condor*. The Bf 109 had all but complete mastery of the air over the Iberian peninsula, sweeping its enemies from the skies, and the German propaganda ministry capitalized with the usual exaggerations. History, however, would prove these exaggerations very accurate, only the statement that the fighter was in "widespread use" was blatantly untrue. In August 1937 only I and II/JG 132 *Richthofen* and I/JG 234 *Schlageter* had Bf 109s and none of these were at full strength, it would be November before a fourth *Gruppe*, II/JG 234, began equipping with the *Berta*.

In fact, as late as 12 March 1938 when the Nazis drove into Austria, the *Luftwaffe* had only 12 *Jagdgruppen* (not counting those in Spain) of which only half had converted or were converting to the Bf 109. Either equipped with or converting to the 109 were:

I/JG131 at Jesau	Bf 109B
I/JG132 at Döberitz	Bf 109B
II/JG132 at Jüterborg-Damm	Bf 109B
I/JG234 at Cologne	Bf 109B
II/JG234 at Düsseldorf	Bf 109B
I/JG334 at Wiesbaden	Bf 109B

Flying other fighters were:

I/JG136 at Eger-Marinbad	He 51C-2
I/JG134 at Dortmund	Ar 68
II/JG134 at Werl	Ar 68
I/JG135 at Aibling	Ar 68
I/JG137 at Bernburg	Ar 68
II/JG133 at Mannheim	Ar 68

Propeller Development

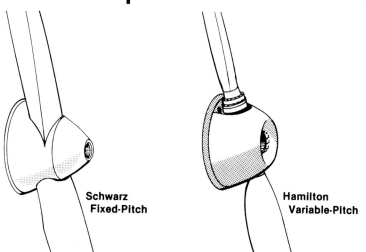

Schwarz
Fixed-Pitch

Hamilton
Variable-Pitch

A brand new Bf 109B-2 equipped with a variable pitch airscrew but not having the three gun cooling slots. The machine is painted in the standard splinter scheme of Black-Green (70) and Dark Green (71) over Light Blue (65) undersurfaces. Still in its infancy, the *Luftwaffe* was mainly concerned with hiding its aircraft on the ground — hence the very dark camouflage scheme fitting to the dark European coniferous forests. (Bundesarchiv)

The second *Gruppe* of the premier *Geschwader* JG 132 *Richthofen* was the first unit to convert to the low-wing fighter and begin working up tactics. Learned from hard experience in Spain, the pair or *Rotte* quickly became the basic *Luftwaffe* formation.

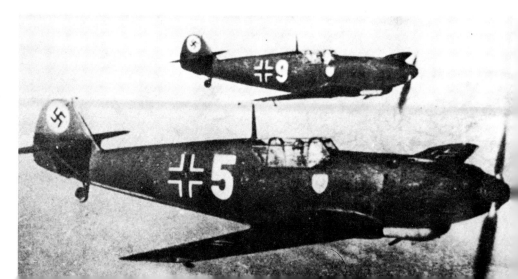

Bf 109C

During early spring of 1938, the **Bf 109C,** which was intended to be the definitive Jumo-powered production aircraft, began replacing the B-series on the production line. Powered by a 700 h.p. fuel injected Jumo 210Ga, the **C-1** had a redesigned exhaust system which featured the addition of short pipes which carried the hot gasses away from the cowling. The addition of fuel injection offered the distinct advantage over a carburation system by being able to function equally as well inverted, or under negative G forces, especially important during a dogfight. Again a centrally mounted weapon was tried without success, a 20mm MG FF/M cannon. As a result, an MG 17 machine gun was installed in each wing just outboard of the wheelwell.

With some of the first batch going to Spain to beef up the *Legion Condor* and service test the new armament, it was summer before I/JG 132, the first homeland unit to receive the C series, had fully exchanged its B-1s for the newer C-1. Neither the **Bf 109C-2** which continued experimenting with the troublesome engine-mounted MG FF cannon, nor the **Bf 109C-3** which tested the MG FF cannon in wing positions, ever went into production.

With the absorption of Austria into the Greater Reich out of the way, Hitler turned his attention to the recovery of the Sudetenland. As tension in Europe increased over the question of Czechoslovakia, the *Jagdgruppen* were increased by no less than eight *Gruppen* on 1 July 1938. Based on newly repainted obsolete aircraft, these *Gruppen* were:

III/JG 132 at Jüterborg-Damm *
IV/JG 132 at Werneuchen
IV/JG 134 at Dortmund
II/JG 135 at Aibling
II/JG 137 at Zerbst
I/JG 138 at Aspern **
III/JG 234 at Düsseldorf
III/JG 334 at Mannheim

* Formed from experienced Austrian Air Force personnel.
** Initially equipped with Ar 68Es this unit shortly received twelve Heinkel He 112B-0s which were originally scheduled for delivery to Japan.

Armament Development

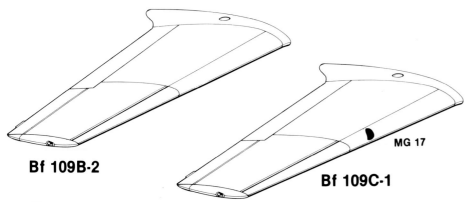

Bf 109B-2

Bf 109C-1

MG 17

The two armorers are replenishing the MG 17 ammunition while the *Obergefreiter* in the foreground adjusts the fuel injection unit first introduced on the Bf 109C-1. This sharkmouthed machine is believed to belong to 2/JG 71 which later became II/JG 51 *Mölders.* **(Bundesarchiv)**

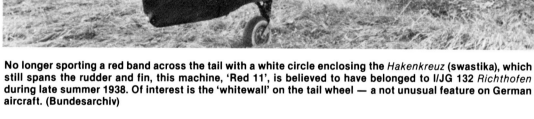

No longer sporting a red band across the tail with a white circle enclosing the *Hakenkreuz* (swastika), which still spans the rudder and fin, this machine, 'Red 11', is believed to have belonged to I/JG 132 *Richthofen* during late summer 1938. Of interest is the 'whitewall' on the tail wheel — a not unusual feature on German aircraft. (Bundesarchiv)

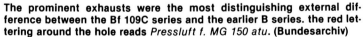

The prominent exhausts were the most distinguishing external difference between the Bf 109C series and the earlier B series. the red lettering around the hole reads *Pressluft f. MG 150 atu*. (Bundesarchiv)

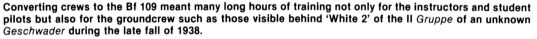

Converting crews to the Bf 109 meant many long hours of training not only for the instructors and student pilots but also for the groundcrew such as those visible behind 'White 2' of the II *Gruppe* of an unknown *Geschwader* during the late fall of 1938.

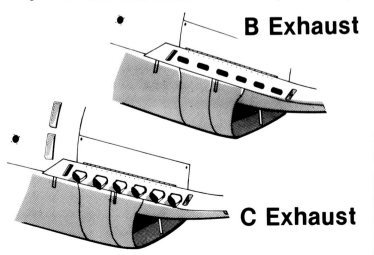

B Exhaust

C Exhaust

Bf 109C-1

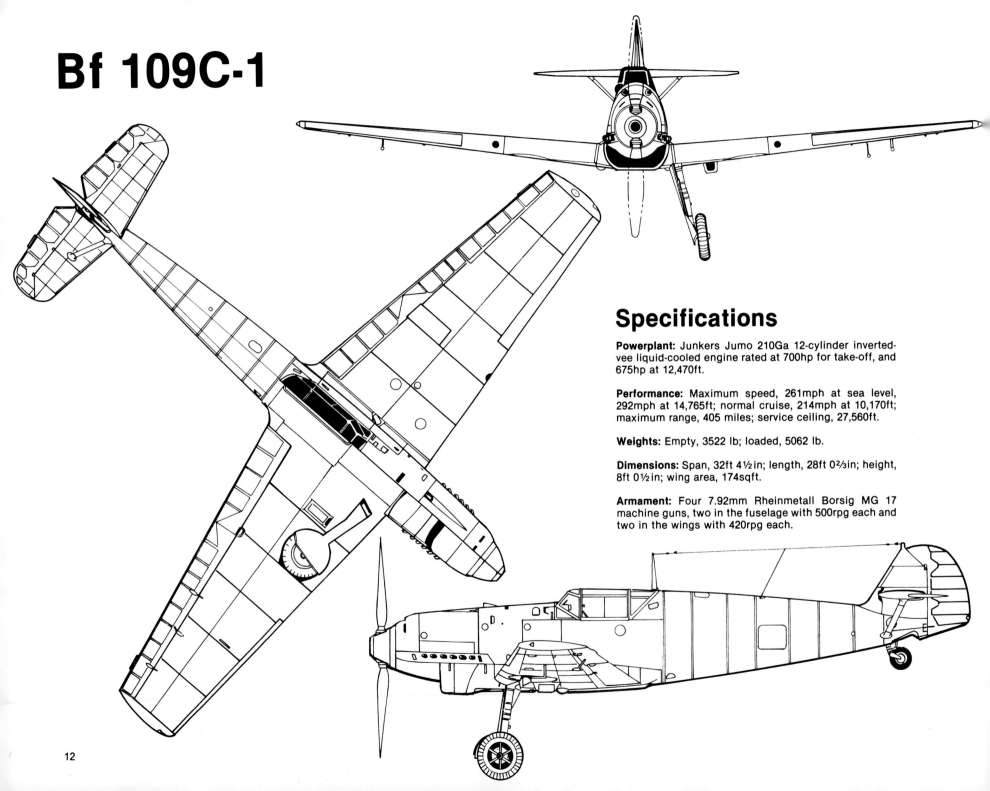

Specifications

Powerplant: Junkers Jumo 210Ga 12-cylinder inverted-vee liquid-cooled engine rated at 700hp for take-off, and 675hp at 12,470ft.

Performance: Maximum speed, 261mph at sea level, 292mph at 14,765ft; normal cruise, 214mph at 10,170ft; maximum range, 405 miles; service ceiling, 27,560ft.

Weights: Empty, 3522 lb; loaded, 5062 lb.

Dimensions: Span, 32ft 4½in; length, 28ft 0⅔in; height, 8ft 0½in; wing area, 174sqft.

Armament: Four 7.92mm Rheinmetall Borsig MG 17 machine guns, two in the fuselage with 500rpg each and two in the wings with 420rpg each.

Bf 109D 'Dora'

In 1934, when the original specifications were issued to the four competing manufacturers, the proviso was made that the Junkers Jumo 210 powerplant would be interchangeable with the more powerful, but less developed Daimler-Benz DB 600 powerplant. It was intended that the **Bf 109D** series would introduce the more powerful Damiler-Benz engine.

Scheduled for the spring of 1938 the planned introduction was delayed for several reasons. First, because it was felt that the bomber force was a great deterrent to Great Britain and France and, since the DB 600 engine also powered the Heinkel He 111, then the backbone of Germany's bomber force, the Heinkel won out. Second, the DB 600 had proven reliable enough to be installed in twin-engine aircraft but wasn't considered reliable enough to be certified for use in single-engine aircraft. Third, Daimler-Benz assured Luftwaffe procurement that serial production of the superior DB 601 powerplant was about to commence.

As always, however, what the Reich's industry could not produce, Göbbel's propaganda ministry invented. In an effort to mislead Germany's enemies into believing that the more powerful and faster DB 600 powered Bf 109D was actually in production, several DB 600 equipped prototypes were photographed in spurious service markings. Other than these machines there is no factual evidence to suggest that a DB 600 *Dora* was serially produced.

What in fact was produced in numbers was an interim Jumo 210Da powered **Bf 109D-1** that was essentially similar to the earlier C series. In anticipation of higher loading, local strengthening was carried out and a heavier main wing spar was introduced, a new cantilever leg for the tail wheel replaced the braced one and a Revi C/12D gunsight was introduced.

Coming off the assembly line during the spring of 1938 the first *Doras* were issued to I/JG 131 at Jesau. By August 1938 the Bf 109 still made up less than half of the Luftwaffe's 643 first-line fighters. Production tempo was such that only seven weeks later Luftwaffe strength reports indicated that 583 Bf 109s were on strength. In anticipation of receiving the twin-engine Bf 110* the *Jagdflieger* was reorganized into *leichten* (light) and *schweren* (heavy) *Jagdgruppen*. On 1 January 1939 the *schweren Jagdgruppen* were redesignated *Zerstörergruppen* and shortly began re-equipping with the Bf 110.

The *Dora* which was essentially the same as the C series with the exception of reverting to the earlier Jumo 210Da, underwent one further development when the exhaust evacuation system was revised on late production D-1 aircraft. It is not known whether this system, externally very similar to the E exhaust system, was a production change or retrofitted to existing aircraft. The author has found no evidence that aircraft with this exhaust system served outside of training units.

* See Squadron/Signal No.1030 Messerschmitt Bf 110 Zerstorer in Action.

Tail Wheel Development

Bf 109C

Bf 109D

This much seen photo has been variously identified as a Bf 109B-2 (William Green) and 'the third 'Dora-series to be delivered to the *Legion Condor*' (Thomas H. Hitchcock). If it is a D-1, the small brace on the tail wheel would indicate that it is one of the very earliest *Doras*. (Hans Obert)

The triangular *VDM* emblem found on each propeller blade of factory fresh aircraft quickly disappeared on service aircraft as the blades became worn and were repainted. The brace on the inside lip of the radiator cowl can be seen, as can the aileron mass balance, tie down ring and pitot tube on the lower port wing. The camouflage is 65/70/71. Note that while it has a soft sprayed edge on the fuselage, it has a hard masked edge where it wraps around the wing leading edge. (Bundesarchiv)

A number of *Doras* were equipped with a flare chute on the starboard side. The braided wire canopy stop can be clearly seen behind the pilot's head. The instrument panel, which can be seen through the window opening, was painted 66 (dark gray) with black instrument faces. (National Archives)

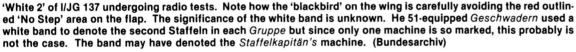

'White 2' of I/JG 137 undergoing radio tests. Note how the 'blackbird' on the wing is carefully avoiding the red outlined 'No Step' area on the flap. The significance of the white band is unknown. He 51-equipped *Geschwadern* used a white band to denote the second *Staffeln* in each *Gruppe* but since only one machine is so marked, this probably is not the case. The band may have denoted the *Staffelkapitän's* machine. (Bundesarchiv)

Three machines belonging to 1/JG 137 *Bernberg* are put through their preflight checks. Besides carrying the *Bernberg Jäger*, this unit also carries a black hand emblem on a surround of white. 1/JG 137 eventually became 1/ZG 2. (Bundesarchiv)

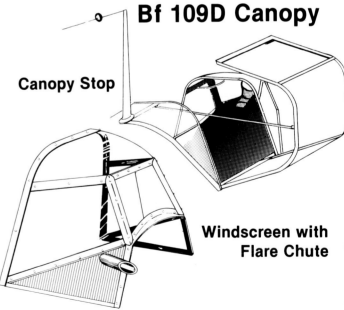

Bf 109D Canopy

Canopy Stop

Windscreen with Flare Chute

The short barrelled MG 17s buried in the wings provided much needed additional firepower since the engine-mounted cannon had proven unsatisfactory. The small oil cooler mounted under the port wing can also be seen to advantage. (Bundesarchiv)

Revi C/12D Gunsight

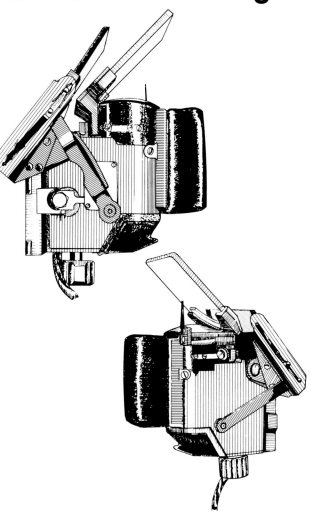

This late Bf 109D-1 with the revised exhaust system is serving with an operational training unit in Denmark, training Slovakian pilots. (Zdenek Titz)

Bf 109E 'Emil'

Because of continued teething troubles and poor reliability of the DB 600 coupled with the manufacturer's confidence that the more powerful DB 601 would be in full production by the summer of 1938, the decision was made to phase out production of the DB 600. The first two **Bf 109D-0** preproduction airframes, redesignated V14 and V15, powered by DB 601A-1 engines rated at 1,050h.p. at take off, began trials during the summer of 1938. Equipped with a Bosch fuel injection system, a preproduction batch of eight **Bf 109E-0** fighters were completed during the fall of 1938 and production airframes were soon ready to come down the assembly line. Before it became obvious that the promised delivery date of production DB 601 powerplants could not be met, E-1 airframes were in fact already coming down the assembly line. Rather than interrupt production, nearly completed airframes were put into storage awaiting engine delivery.

Essentially similar to its predecessor aft of the firewall, the Emil incorporated a completely redesigned lower cowling section into which the oil cooler was moved; the chin radiator was moved to the wings where two shallow glycol radiators were provided. As with the C and D, E-1 armament was standardized on a pair of cowling-mounted MG 17s and a pair of wing-mounted MG 17s. Surprisingly, even though pilot armor protection was encountered in the Russian I-16 over Spain, no such protection was provided for either pilot or fuel tankage.

It was not until some six months later than scheduled that the DB 601 was finally certified for single-seat fighter installation. When delivery of the power plants finally did begin, large numbers of the new fighter very quickly became available to the *Jagdgruppen* with deliveries being made to the *Legion Condor* simultaneously. Throughout the spring and summer of 1939 the *Jagdstaffeln* worked feverishly to convert to the new fighter.

As badly as the Luftwaffe needed the new fighter, the Reich apparently needed hard currency more. During the winter of 1938-39 Switzerland was allowed to purchase 10 Jumo-powered Bf 109s and placed an order for thirty Bf 109E-1s. On 14 April 1939 the first of the *Emils* were delivered and Swiss authorities, obviously very impressed with their new machines, immediately supplemented their previous order with an order for an additional fifty!

During the whole of 1938 Bf 109 production just barely crept over the 400 mark. However, with the introduction of the DB powered E series the production tempo increased to such an extent that nearly 1100 aircraft were delivered during the first eight months of 1939. During this period fighters were being delivered almost faster than the *Jagdgruppen* could absorb them. The *Luftwaffe* at last had its first-line fighter, a fighter that was equal to or better than any fighter in the world, a fighter that certainly was better than anything manufactured in continental Europe, a fighter with which Germany could go to war.

On 23 August Germany and Russia publically signed a non-aggression pact, in which they secretly divided up Poland. Eight days later Germany struck across Polish borders with massive air and land forces.

The Bf 109E-1 featured a completely redesigned and much more aerodynamically streamlined lower cowling. The single large radiator bath under the engine was supplanted by two small glycol radiators under the wings and the small underwing oil cooler was moved under the engine. (Bundesarchiv)

Cowling Development

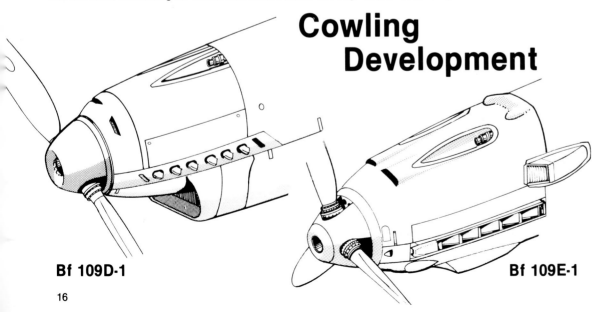

Bf 109D-1

Bf 109E-1

'Yellow 9', a Bf 109E-1 belonging to JG 132 *Richthofen,* sports yellow wargames crosses. As Nazi demands upon Europe increased and tensions continued to mount, military exercises took on more sinister meaning.

A few of the early E-1s were also equipped with the flare chute on the starboard side of the canopy. (Bundesarchiv)

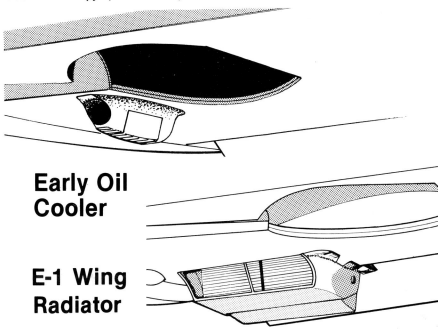

Early Oil Cooler

E-1 Wing Radiator

The wing mounted MG 17s carried by the E-1 series were unchanged from the *Dora* series. The as yet unidentified emblem is believed to be associated with JG 53. Of particular interest is the non-standard rearview mirror fitted to this machine. (Bundesarchiv)

'Yellow 2', an E-1 of JG 21 (later JG 54) illustrates the standard color scheme of the *Tag Jagd* (Day Fighter) at this time. Still fearful of a surprise attack which could catch their aircraft on the ground, all surfaces which could be seen from the air were painted in Dark Green (71)/Black Green (70) with Light Blue (65) undersurfaces. A holdover from when the swastika was centered on a circle of white in a red band, the Nazi symbol is here painted overlapping the fin and rudder. (Obert)

Believing the threat of Allied attack on their airfields to be a very real possibility, realistic wooden dummies were constructed and strategically placed. Sort of one-to-one scale models. (Smithsonian)

Poland

Contrary to popular opinion, just over 200 Bf 109s participated in the opening phases of the invasion of Poland:

I. (Jagd)/LG 2	39 Bf 109Es
II./ZG 1	36 Bf 109Bs
I./JG 1	54 Bf 109Es
I./JG 21	29 Bf 109C & Es
I./ZG 2	44 Bf 109Ds

All other Bf 109 units, a number of which were still undergoing conversion to the new fighter, remained in Germany concentrated along the western frontier as a defense against interference from either the RAF or the *Armee de l' Air*. Total *Luftwaffe* strength for Operation *Ostmark* has been surrounded by controversy, with the total variously being set at between 1500 and 3000 aircraft. Opposing the *Luftwaffe* was less than 200 obsolete PZL P.11 and P.7 fighters. One of the first air battles occured over Warsaw when 30 PZLs intercepted He 111s of KG 27 protected by Bf 109Es and Bf 110s. A number of PZLs were shot down. A Bf 109 was lost when it was rammed by a Polish fighter. What had been first demonstrated in Spain was now vividly brought home in the skies over Poland. German fighters would seldom be able to engage in WW I style dogfights. Due to the much greater speed of the Bf 109; either a fighter pilot was in a good position to attack at high speed or he went in search of fairer game.

The Polish defences fought courageously, costing the *Luftwaffe* over one hundred aircraft for a loss of seventy-nine Polish aircraft during the first six days of the war. After the 7th, however, German mastery of the air was all but total, and the Bf 109s went over to the ground-attack role, mainly strafing troop concentrations. The 67 Bf 109s that were shot down during the Polish campaign were mainly lost during this period, falling victim to ground fire.

Poland's end became inevitable when Russia invaded Eastern Poland on 17 August. The Polish Government and High Command took refuge in Romania on the 18th, with Warsaw holding out until the 27th.

A *Rottenfuhrer* and his wingman doublecheck coordinates before a sortie over the battlefield. (Bundesarchiv)

'Red 7' of I/JG 1, having been refueled and rearmed, is about to take off on another mission. This *Jagdgruppe* was pulled out of the Polish campaign early and sent to the Western border to perform guard duty.

A Bf 109C-1 of 3/JG 21 (later 9/JG 54) at Gutenfeld/East Prussia early in the Polish Campaign. The rings on the spinner are in the 3. *Staffel* color of yellow. The wheels, which appear to be painted black, are in fact Gray (66), a very dark color. (K. Ries)

Bf 109E
Seat

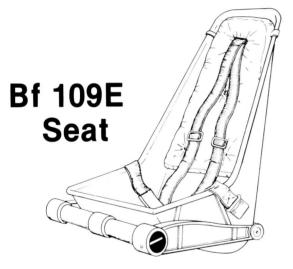

(Above Right) This E-1 of JG 21 that bellied in, seems to have some damage near the oil reserve tank. The prop was turning as the pilot touched down as evidenced by the bent blades. The pilot, being able to bring the machine back to an airfield, meant that the aircraft could usually be made airworthy in a few days. (Obert)

Another downed machine belonging to JG 21 is the subject of much curious examination by ground forces. Most of the 67 Bf 109s lost during the Polish Campaign were victims of ground fire. (Bundesarchiv)

Sitzkrieg

On 3 September Britain and France, fulfilling their treaty obligations to Poland, declared war on Germany. The so-called phony war or *Sitzkrieg* (sitting war) as the Germans called it, had begun along the Western Front. Inaction on the ground however was not reflected in the air where a real, shooting war very quickly developed.

On 4 September the Bf 109 had the singular honor of drawing first RAF blood when Fw. Held and Fw. Troitsch of II/JG 77, flying Bf 109E-1s, claimed a Wellington each from a force attacking *Scharnhorst* and *Gneisenau* off Brunsbüttel. Although Held was widely acclaimed in the German Press as having shot down the first Tommy, Carl Schumacher, who commanded II/JG 77 at the time, always believed Troitsch actually brought down the first RAF bomber. On 30 September Bf 109E-1s of JG 53 brought down four out of five Fairey Battles of No. 150 Squadron carrying out an armed reconnaissance over Saarbrücken.

Meanwhile *Armee De L'Air* fighters and the *Jagdgruppen* constantly clashed while intruding into each other's airspace. On 8 September, five Hawk 75s engaged a like number of Bf 109s, claiming two shot down in the first fighter vs. fighter combat on the Western Front. During September the French claimed 27 German aircraft for a loss of only eight of their own.

As jubilant air and ground crewmen gather around, the finishing touches are added to the first victory marking on Fw. Alfred Held's rudder. (Bundesarchiv)

Flying 'Red 1', Fw. Held of 5/JG 77 sweeps in across the beach at Wangerooge Island after a patrol of the Heligoland Bight area. (Bundesarchiv)

Fw. Held had flown with 4 J/88 in Spain and carried the Spanish top hat as his personal insignia as well as the seagull emblem of 5/JG 77.

When five Fairey Battles of No. 150 Squadron carried out an armed reconnaissance over Saarbrücken, four of them were shot down. (Bundesarchiv)

Bf 109E Cockpit

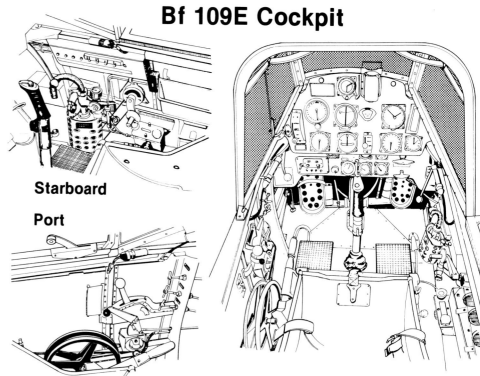

Starboard

Port

(Above Left) The overall 70/71 upper surfaces did nothing to hide the aircraft in the air. (Obert)

Bf 109E-1s of JG 132 *Schlageter* warm up prior to a patrol along the Franco-German border during the *Sitzkrieg*. JG 132 will shortly be redesignated JG 26. (Obert)

Lt. Hubert Kroeck, a *Legion Condor* veteran, lectures young pilots of JG 53 *Pik As* on air fighting tactics. Kroeck's machine carries a top hat, his personal insignia. (Bundesarchiv)

While the *Sitzkrieg* was punctuated by sharp clashes, it provided plenty of time for recreation. This aircraft, an E-1 belonging to 1/JG 77, demonstrates the new lighter scheme which came into use late in 1939. No longer afraid of being caught on the ground, more concerned with being seen in the air, Lt. Blue (65) was painted high up the sides of Bf 109s. The spinner and propeller blades are painted Black-Green (70). The camouflage net is not a net as such, but stretched wire with faggots of weeds and straw attached. (Bundesarchiv)

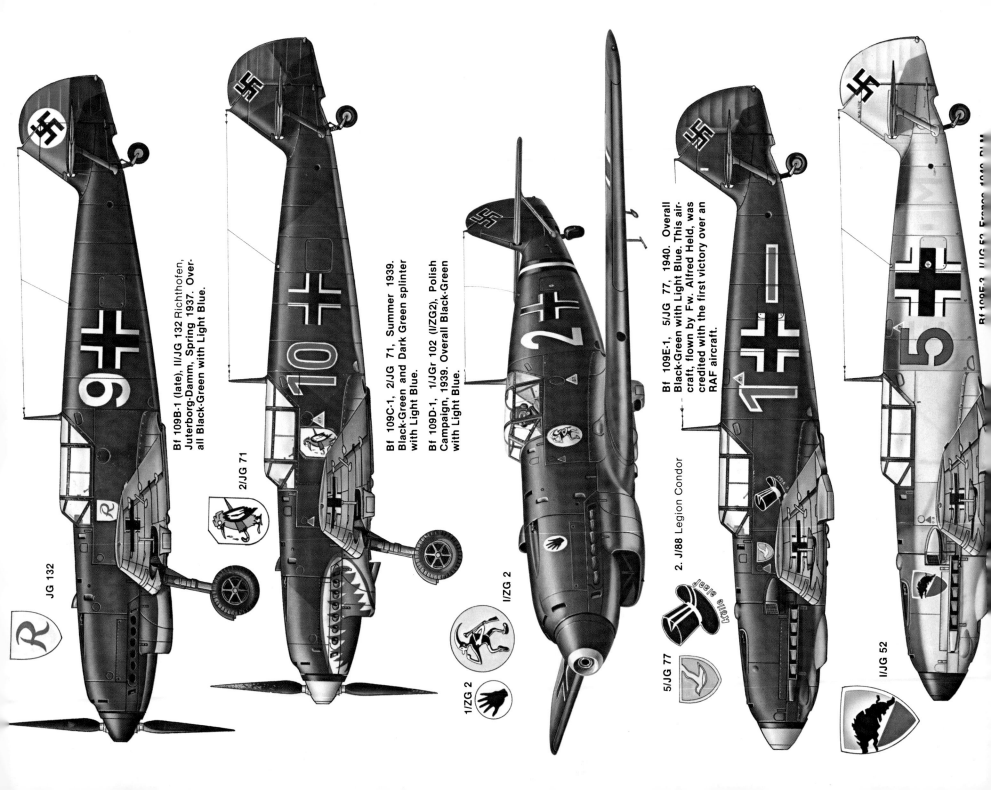

Bf 109B-1 (late), II/JG 132 Richthofen, Juterborg-Damm, Spring 1937. Overall Black-Green with Light Blue.

JG 132

2/JG 71

Bf 109C-1, 2/JG 71, Summer 1939. Black-Green and Dark Green splinter with Light Blue.

Bf 109D-1, 1/JGr 102 (I/ZG2), Polish Campaign, 1939. Overall Black-Green with Light Blue.

I/ZG 2

1/ZG 2

2. J/88 Legion Condor

Bf 109E-1, 5/JG 77, 1940. Overall Black-Green with Light Blue. This aircraft, flown by Fw. Alfred Held, was credited with the first victory over an RAF aircraft.

5/JG 77

I/JG 52

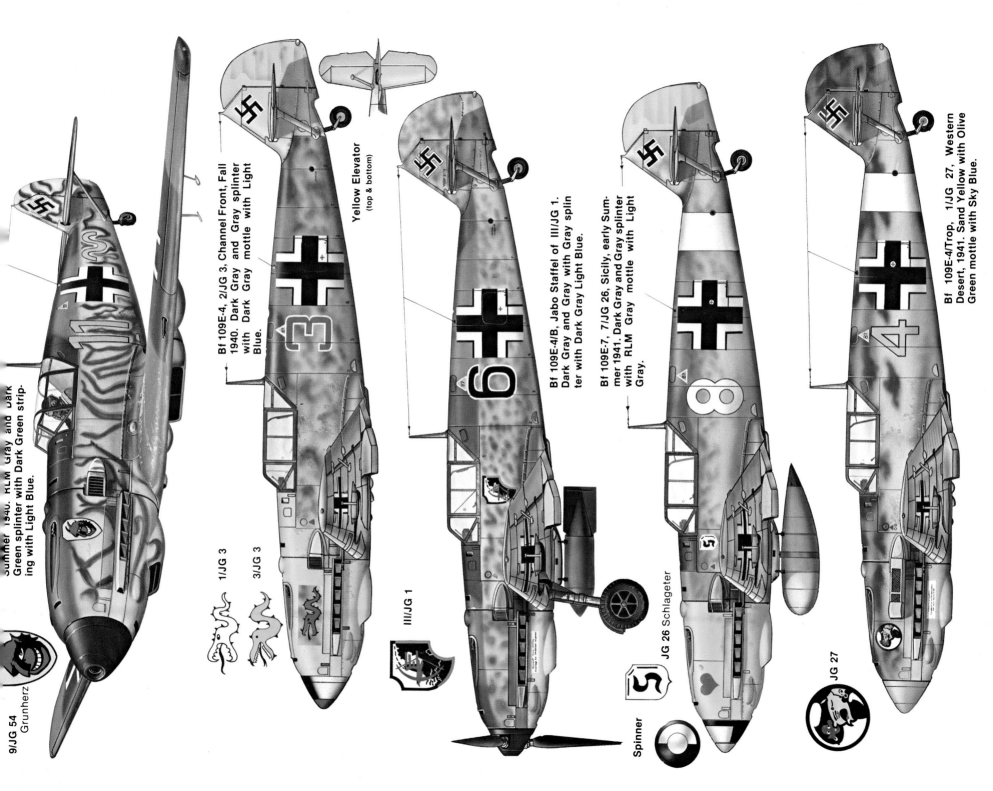

Summer 1940. RLM Gray and Dark Green splinter with Dark Green striping with Light Blue.

9/JG 54
Grunherz

Bf 109E-4, 2/JG 3, Channel Front, Fall 1940. Dark Gray and Gray splinter with Dark Gray mottle with Light Blue.

1/JG 3
3/JG 3

Yellow Elevator
(top & bottom)

Bf 109E-4/B, Jabo Staffel of III/JG 1. Dark Gray and Gray with Gray splinter with Dark Gray Light Blue.

III/JG 1

Bf 109E-7, 7/JG 26, Sicily, early Summer 1941. Dark Gray and Gray splinter with RLM Gray mottle with Light Gray.

Spinner

JG 26 Schlageter

Bf 109E-4/Trop, 1/JG 27, Western Desert, 1941. Sand Yellow with Olive Green mottle with Sky Blue.

JG 27

Bf 109E-3

During the early fall of 1939, the *Jagdgruppen* received the more heavily armed **Bf 109E-3**. The **Bf 109E-2** had been another unsuccessful attempt at introducing the engine mounted MG FF cannon. Again vibration and jamming of the engine-mounted weapon caused its rejection. A handful of these machines were believed to have been produced and there is evidence that suggests II/JG 27 operated a few of this type.

Continued development of the Daimler powerplant resulted in the DB 601Aa-powered Bf 109E-3. Again provision was made for the installation of an engine-mounted cannon and again it was found to be unsatisfactory; those few delivered with the engine-mounted armament invariably had them removed. Very early in the production run the wing mounted MG 17 machine guns were replaced by 20mm MG FF cannons, the greater bulk of which necessitated a bulged plate being added to the underwing. Not only did the E-3 series possess much heavier firepower as a result, but maximum speed was increased from 334 mph to 348 mph.

Bf 109E-3s began arriving at the *Jagdgruppen* during the autumn of 1939 with II/JG 54 receiving some of the first machines. On 22 November an E-3 fell into Allied hands when a pilot from II/JG 54 crashlanded near Worth, some twenty miles inside France. This machine would not only be tested by the French but was in turn sent to England and eventually to the U.S. for evaluation. The new, faster and harder-punching aircraft were extremely welcome to the young *Luftwaffe* pilots that, on occasion, were literally fighting for their lives against Allied pilots.

On 22 November, an E-3 fell into Allied hands when a pilot of JG 54 crash landed near Worth. That same day, Lt. Helmut Wick of I/JG 53, flying an E-1, did battle with four Hawk 75s, downing one of them.

Armament Development

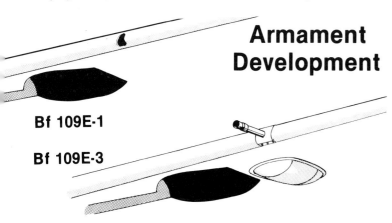

Bf 109E-1

Bf 109E-3

The downed Bf 109E-3 of JG 54 was put on display at a Paris department store. One of the earliest E-3s, it was equipped with wing mounted MG 17 machine guns rather than 20mm cannons.

This E-3 belonging to 1/JG 2 clearly shows the camouflage and markings of the Bf 109E in transition. The Lt. Blue (65) has been extended up the fuselage sides as per the latest instructions. However, the early style fuselage cross with the narrow white edges has been retained as well as the old style position of the swastika. Note that the upper wing cross is located much further out on the wing than the later, more central position. (Obert)

Main Landing Gear

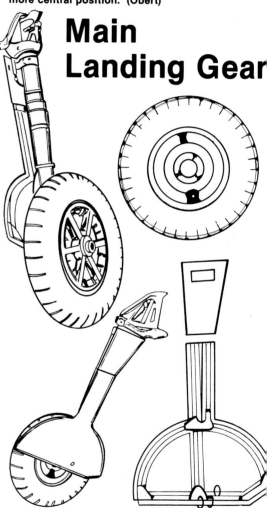

As the hard winter of 1939-40 set in, flying time was greatly reduced. These E-3s carry the new style, high visibility crosses that allowed the *Jagdstaffeln* to quickly recognize friend from foe in the air.

Bf 109E-3

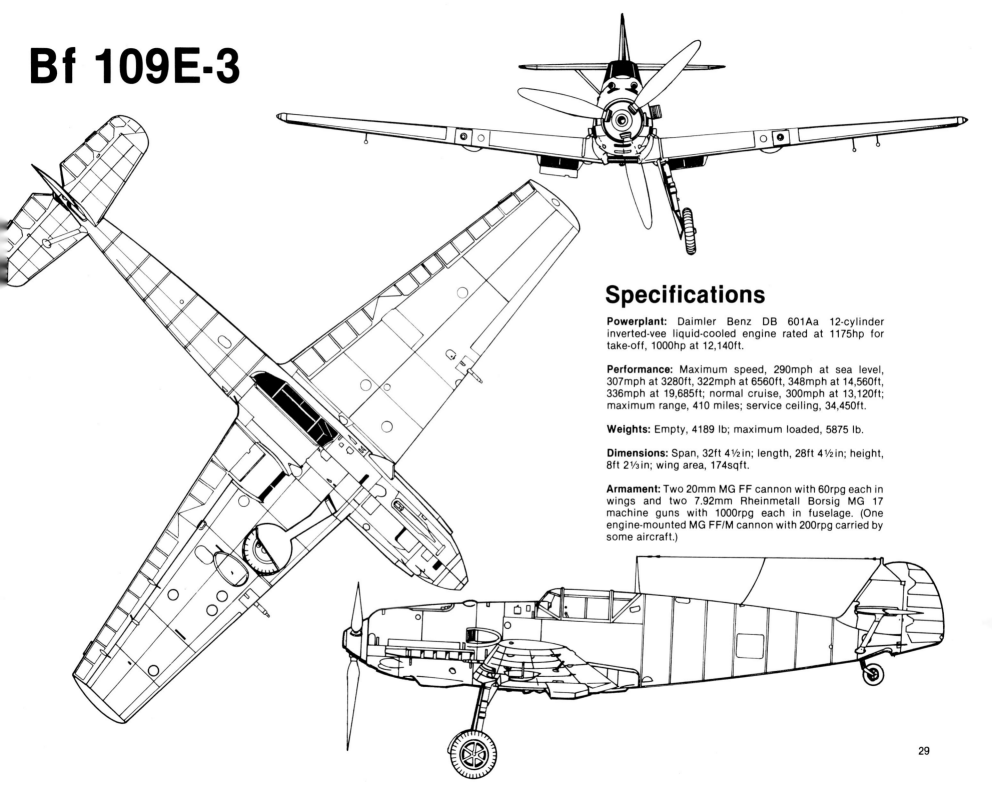

Specifications

Powerplant: Daimler Benz DB 601Aa 12-cylinder inverted-vee liquid-cooled engine rated at 1175hp for take-off, 1000hp at 12,140ft.

Performance: Maximum speed, 290mph at sea level, 307mph at 3280ft, 322mph at 6560ft, 348mph at 14,560ft, 336mph at 19,685ft; normal cruise, 300mph at 13,120ft; maximum range, 410 miles; service ceiling, 34,450ft.

Weights: Empty, 4189 lb; maximum loaded, 5875 lb.

Dimensions: Span, 32ft 4½in; length, 28ft 4½in; height, 8ft 2⅓in; wing area, 174sqft.

Armament: Two 20mm MG FF cannon with 60rpg each in wings and two 7.92mm Rheinmetall Borsig MG 17 machine guns with 1000rpg each in fuselage. (One engine-mounted MG FF/M cannon with 200rpg carried by some aircraft.)

Assault on the West

By late spring of 1940 the *Jagdgruppen* could claim nearly a thousand Bf 109E-1s and E-3s on strength, the earlier B, C and Ds having been relegated to such second-line roles as nightfighting or training. On 9 April the *Sitzkrieg* came to an end when the German juggernaut attacked Denmark and Norway in order to effectively seal off the eastern portion of the North Sea. The shipment of iron ore from Sweden to the Reich would be shielded from interference by Allied sea power. The only Bf 109-equipped unit to participate in the action was II/JG 77.

On 10 May 1940 the *Luftwaffe* committed sixteen *Gruppen* of Bf 109Es from nine *Geschwaders,* JG 1, 2, 3, 21, 26, 27, 51, 53 and 54, (JG 77 being busy in Norway); nearly a thousand Bf 109Es out of a total 3900 aircraft supporting German ground forces which quickly overran Holland, Belgium and Luxemburg. On the 14th Holland surrendered after a 100,000 casualties, her airforce being knocked out after the first day of fighting. By the 14th Von Kleist's panzers, having simply bypassed the Maginot Line, opened a fifty mile front west of Sedan. Guderian pushed his men and armor hard, reaching the Atlantic on the 20th and effectively isolating the British Expeditionary Force. Ground forces immediately began tightening the circle around the beleagered Allied forces. Cutoff from the large French army, Allied troops, French, Belgian, Dutch and English, began to fall back toward Dunkirk, where the decision was made to evacuate them.

From the opening, the *Luftwaffe's* superiority in the air was in little doubt, although occassionally French and English squadrons would gain the upper hand. British and French pilots fought courageously but due to the rapidly moving ground battle, Allied air units repeatedly had to abandon bases and equipment or face capture. Allied airfields, logistics and communications were constantly under attack with more Allied fighters being lost to strafing and abandonment than were lost in actual combat. And combat was fierce and determined, on 14 May JG 53 alone claimed 39 kills. Many of the veterens who would become battle-tested air leaders throughout the coming war years got their first kills during this period; Adolph Galland, Gunther Rall, Max-Hellmuth Osterkamp, to mention only a few.

As the fighting closed around Dunkirk, the *Jagdfleiger,* its supply lines stretched taut, began to feel the attrition which the previous two weeks of constant fighting had taken on men and aircraft. While actual combat losses were only some 147 fighter aircraft during the whole of May, with a further 88 damaged, serviceability was becoming a problem — spare parts and even fuel became critical for some units. The panzer units closing a noose of iron around Dunkirk were in much the same situation, many units were operating at less than half strength, fuel and ammunition were both in short supply and to the south nearly two-thirds of the French army, if somewhat disorganized, was still intact.

On 24 May Hitler ordered the Panzer Divisions halted. Göring, however, boasted that his Luftwaffe alone could destroy the British at Dunkirk from the air and prevent their evacuation. On 23 and 24 May the Bf 109 was to meet its mortal enemy — the Spitfire — for the first time, a nemesis that would dog it for all of its combat days. During these initial encounters the Messerschmitt fighter came out about even. However, in a dogfight just south of Dunkirk, No. 92 Squadron, flying its first operational sortie, claimed to have met six Bf 109s, destroying all of them for the loss of only one of their own. While it is felt these claims, made during the heat of battle, were probably exaggerated, Luftwaffe pilots found that for the first time they were up against a well-trained enemy possessing an aircraft equal to their own.

Believing that there was no way off the beaches for the several hundred thousand Allied troops, Göring's attack was slow to develop. However, since 20 May, the British Admiralty had been assembling a huge fleet of small vessels; tugs, motor launches, paddle steamers, yachts, any vessel, civilian or military, that was capable of crossing the Channel. Under the code name 'Dynamo', the ragtag armada was ordered to begin evacuating troops from Dunkirk. That same night Guderian was ordered to resume the Panzer assault.

The brief halt by German ground forces allowed almost 340,000 trapped Allied troops to escape to Great Britain. Because the *Jagdstaffeln,* at a low level after several weeks of combat, had not been able to fight through the umbrella of Spitfires over Dunkirk, the *Luftwaffe's* bomber force suffered their first mauling.

On 5 June the *Blitzkrieg* turned south, knifing into France. Paris was declared an open city on 12 June with Marshall Petain asking for an armistice on the 17th.

With nearly a thousand Bf 109s in the air, all too often this was the last sight seen by an English or French pilot, a *Rotte* of *Emils.* The lead aircraft is an E-3 with the underwing MG FF cannon bulges clearly visible, while the wingman's aircraft is an E-1.

I/JG 53 *Pik As* by nightfall of 14 May had collected some 39 kills, 10 of them belonging to Hauptmann Werner Mölders. JG 53 was one of the few units to carry the 70/71 splinter pattern overall on its upper surfaces into the French Campaign. (Bundesarchiv)

No matter how hectic or how fast the movement became, ground crewmen always seemed to have time to add the victory markings to their charges.

(Above Left) Flying sortie after sortie, flying personnel were often times on the ground only long enough to grab a bite to eat, refuel and re-arm their machines. Operational demands were such that normal required maintenance had to be done after dark, when it was nearly impossible, or be let go for 'another day'. These 'blackbirds' are re-arming the cowl-mounted MG 17 magazines. (Bundesarchiv)

During the early field-hopping behind the rapidly advancing *Panzers*, ground personnel dug the required slit trenches. However, as the *Jagdstafeln* moved from field to field, sometime after only hours, slit trenches were seen less frequently. (Bundesarchiv)

This pilot of III/JG 27 looks like he would rather be doing almost anything other than waiting for the mechanics to make an engine adjustment before he can join his comrades already in the air. During the battle of France this unit began painting the aircraft numeral on the cowling, against regulations, and continued to do so into 1943. (Bundesarchiv)

Looking Across the Channel

Not able to stop the evacuation of Dunkirk solely with his *Luftwaffe*, Göring felt this was the time to invade England. On 5 June the *Feldmarshal* held a conference aboard his armored train outlining a plan that he wanted to take to the *Führer:*

> Five Army divisions to reinforce the existing parachute divisions plus five further divisions organized into his six division Airborne Corps. The *Luftwaffe* fighters, bombers and transports would be brought to an immediate state of readiness. By using these forces the entire Royal Navy and Royal Air Force would be forced to the Channel and into a fight to the finish. The *Luftwaffe* could then be used to destroy them.
> At the end of these decisive battles both sides would have found themselves without anything left, and then, with our reserves, with a mere handful of the 5th and 6th Airborne Divisions, we would bring about the final decision.
>
> Hermann Göring

Hitler rejected any plan to immediately invade England and began putting out peace feelers, hoping the British would realize that the game was lost. No-one in the *Luftwaffe* had the slightest idea that the English would not immediately accept such a magnanimous offer. The pilots at the *Jagdstaffeln* were ready to go 'Home to the *Reich'* to receive their richly deserved honors. Then the impossible happened: the British said, "No!". General reaction among the *Luftwaffe* was that it was ". . .impossible. How could the Tommies be so crazy. They've been defeated but won't give up! Now what?" The front-line pilots were of course just as enthusiastic about coming to grips with the RAF as they were about going home in glory, perhaps a bit more so.

Göring's personal train, in which he outlined his suicidal plan to invade England. Given the state of the English forces at the time, Göring's plan just might have worked. (Barlow)

As the French Campaign drew to a close, armor protection for the pilot was added to the cockpit of the E-3. Easily retrofitted to existing E-1 and E-3 aircraft, 53 lbs. of 8mm armor was added to the seat and 28.6 lbs. of armor was added behind and above the pilot's head in a curved plate that attached to the canopy frame. (Obert)

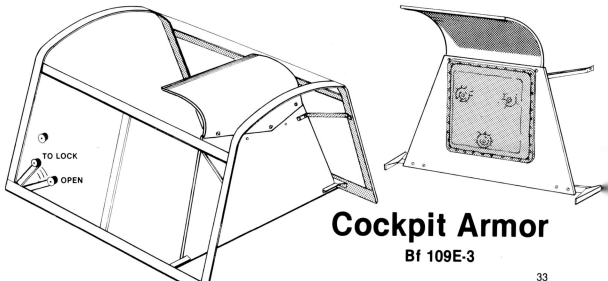

TO LOCK

OPEN

Cockpit Armor
Bf 109E-3

To relieve their own shortage of trained personnel, the *Luftwaffe* immediately began recruiting French civilian airframe mechanics who usually lived near the former French Air Force bases and were quite willing to ply their trade for their new masters, especially after considering the alternatives.

(Above Left) After nearly seven weeks of constant operations, the Bf 109s were in serious need of overhaul. The lull at the end of the French Campaign was put to good use. Here 'Red 14', an E-1, gets extensive and loving care by her ground crew.

'Red 10', also an E-1 undergoes armament calibration preparatory to test firing its quartet of MG 17s. This view affords an excellent view of the automatic leading edge slots. (Bundesarchiv)

Bf 109E-4

As the *Luftwaffe* and RAF sat facing each other across the Channel, the **Bf 109E-4,** incorporating lessons learned in the Polish and French Campaigns, began to enter service. A redesigned canopy with heavier framing was added. The decision to terminate the engine mounted MG FF/M cannon was made and a pair of MG FF/M cannons with improved rate of fire replaced the earlier MG FFs in the wings. Essentially the same as the E-4 and running on the assembly line concurrently with the E-4 was the **Bf 109E-5,** a reconnaissance version having the wing cannon deleted and an RB 21/18 camera mounted in the fuselage.

The **Bf 109E-5/N** which differed from the standard E-4 by being powered by a DB 601N engine came into service just after the French Campaign ended. Compression was increased from 6.9 to 8.2 and 96 octane C3 fuel was required instead of the standard 87 octane B4 fuel. The new powerplant boosted horsepower to 1200 and provided an emergency output of 1270 h.p. for one minute at 16,400 feet.

The **Bf 109E-6** was a makeshift reconnaissance model of the E-3 equipped with a DB 601N engine, the earlier 4 × MG 17s, and a hand-held camera. It is virtually impossible to identify photgraphically.

This early Bf 109E-4 serving with III/JG 54 *Grunherz* along the Channel coast, does not have the canopy-mounted armor plate. (Barlow)

The improved 20mm MG FF/M cannon, mounted in each wing of the E-4 series, is inspected by *Simba,* the mascot of II/JG 3. (Bundesarchiv)

To help distinguish friend from foe during the heat of the battle, a temporary distemper paint, usually either white or yellow, was often applied to the cowling and/or tail. The above Bf 109E-3 belonging to 8/JG 51 has had all fuselage surfaces forward of the wing painted yellow.

As the *Luftwaffe* and the RAF parried with each other over the Channel, camouflage on the 109 began going through another metamorphosis. Again concerned with being attacked on the ground, darker colors were applied along the fuselage sides over Lt. Blue. This machine, 'Red 4' of II/JG2 *Richthofen,* has had a heavy mottle of RLM Gray (02) and Dark Green (71) sponged onto the basic 65/71/02 scheme. (Zdenek Titz)

Canopy Development

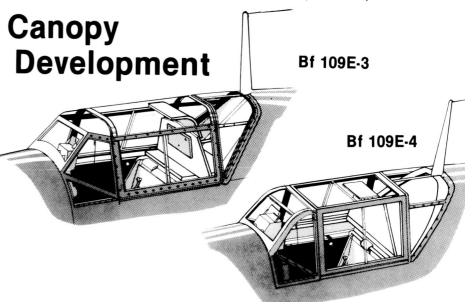

Bf 109E-3

Bf 109E-4

After German forces occupied the Channel Islands, Bf 109s were based at La Villiaze Airfield, Guernsey. This Bf 109E-4 of II/JG 53 *Pik As* is being refueled by J.H. Miller Ltd. As in France, after considering the alternatives, the locals reluctantly did what they were told. (Bundesarchiv)

The E-5 reconnaissance fighter, which was produced in small numbers at the same time as the E-4 fighter, reverted to the wing-mounted MG 17s and carried a fuselage mounted Rb 21/18 camera that shot through an aperture in the belly just behind the wing.

This heavily mottled E-5 reconnaissance fighter belongs to 7/JG 77. The third *Gruppe's* emblem, a black wolf's head on a white shield, is partially visible on the cowling.

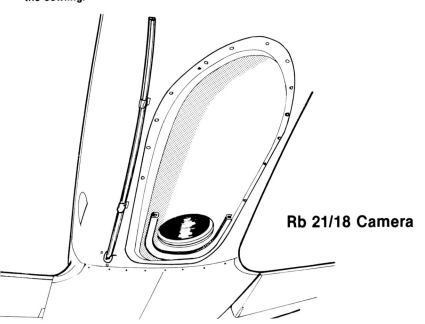

Rb 21/18 Camera

Another E-5 serving with JG 77 having its cowl mounted MG 17s rearmed. The spinner has a nonstandard, and rather odd, pointed shape to it.

Bf 109E-4/B Jabo

During the French Campaign it was decided to employ the Bf 109E as a *Jagdbomber* (Fighter/Bomber). Successful tests were conducted using a rudimentary bombrack mounted beneath the fuselage employing an electrical release gear. Under the command of Hauptmann Walter Rubensdörfer, E.Gr. 210* was charged with service evaluation and working up tactics. Under the designation **Bf 109E-4/B** the *Jabos* equipped 3. *Staffel/E.Gr.* 210, 1. and 2. *Staffel* being equipped with Bf 110C-4/B *Jabos*, beginning operations against Channel targets during July.

* *Erprobungsgruppe 210* was originally formed to introduce the Me 210 into service, which was cancelled.

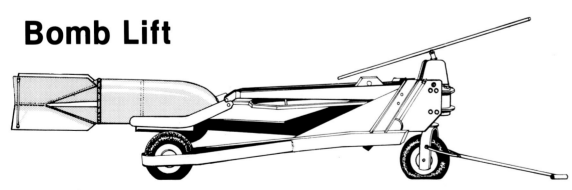

3/*Erprobungsgruppe 210* **was so successful using their Bf 109E-4/Bs that each Geschwader was ordered to form a** *Jabo Staffel.* **The above machine belongs to III/JG 1. (Bundesarchiv)**

Bomb Lift

A special hand-operated lift was provided that allowed one man to hand a SC250 bomb onto an ETC 500 bomb rack. The bomb is painted RLM Gray (02) (a light greenish-gray). At this time, bombs also appeared painted blue, brown or pale yellow. (Bundesarchiv)

Battle of Britain

Across the Channel, the losses suffered by RAF Fighter Command during the forty days of fighting on the continent had been staggering, 509 fighters having been lost. Fortunately for the RAF, few of those fighters lost had been Spitfires, which had been stubbornly retained for home defense. With no clearcut plan of attack, the *Jagdstaffeln* now began *Freijagd* patrols over the Channel and along the Kent coast, aggressively looking for trouble and trying to bring up RAF fighters. Occasionally small formations of bombers, both escorted and unescorted, would attack Channel targets. Few casualties were inflicted by either side in this early sparring and, although the *Jagdstaffein* brought down more enemy fighters, battle losses by either fighter force could be counted on one hand. Poor weather played a large part in keeping the two forces apart during early July and replacement aircraft and maintainance units were quickly making good the *Luftwaffe's* previous seven weeks' losses.

While this re-equipping was going on, the *Luftwaffe* was ordered to close the Channel to English shipping as prelude to the invasion, which would come about as soon as the RAF was eliminated. The destruction of the RAF was to be accomplished by destroying those fighters posted south of a line through Gloucester and then moving the line progressively northward until the U.K. was purged of fighter opposition. To accomplish this, the *Luftwaffe* began massing some 2600 aircraft along the French, Dutch, Belgian and Norwegian coasts. By 20 July, Bf 109-equipped units had been brought back up to 80% of their pre-French campaign strength possessing some 809 aircraft, of which 656 were serviceable.

Emils of II(*Schlacht*)/LG 2 at Calais-Marck are being bombed up for a mission across the Channel. The first and third machines are E-4/Bs, while the middle machine is an E-1 which has been retrofitted with a bomb rack, becoming an E-1/B. (Barlow)

ETC 500 Bomb Rack

Pilots of JG 27 lounge in the bright summer sunlight as their *Emils* are being serviced prior to another mission over the Channel. On 8 August this unit was mauled, losing 11 aircraft. (Barlow)

On 2 August the final operational order for *Adlerangriff* (Attack of the Eagles) was issued with *Adler Tag* (Eagle Day) being set for 10 August, weather permitting. Some authors have pointed to 8 August as being the actual beginning of the Battle of Britain because of the ferocity of the air battle which cost JG 27 eleven Bf 109s on this day alone. Be that as it may, the *Luftwaffe's* full-fledged attack was not scheduled until the 10th. Saturday the 10th, however, was scratched because of weather and while raids were carried out on the 11th it certainly was not up to numbers envisioned for *Adlertag*. Finally on the morning of Tuesday 13 August, Adlertag was to be launched. In the event, only a single formation of bombers were in fact to carry out an attack. Only in the afternoon did the attack finally materialize, but in much smaller numbers than Göring had envisioned. The RAF claimed 64 aircraft and the *Luftwaffe* 84. In fact, British losses were 13 and the *Luftwaffe* 47 including nine Bf 109s. A further 47 British aircraft were destroyed on the ground but only one of these was a fighter. On the 15th, a day which has been dubbed 'Black Thursday' by the *Luftwaffe,* over 2000 sorties were flown against the U.K. and over 50 aircraft were lost, mostly bombers. Those Bf 110 Zerstörers escorting the bombers were shot to pieces and the Bf 110 equipped Stab/Erpr.Gr. 210 attacking Croydon was almost wiped out with Rubensdörfer himself being killed. Only seven Bf 109s were lost including an E-4/B of 3./Erpr.Gr. 210.

During the opening phases of the 'Battle', the *Jagdgruppen* were mainly employed in *'Freijagd'* (free hunting), missions, scouring the countryside for RAF fighters. Using the paired, or *'Rotte',* tactics evolved during the Spanish Civil War, the Bf 109s were often able to bounce the tight three-plane formation still used by the RAF. Eventually Fighter Command tactics began to imitate those of the *Jagdgruppen.* However, as it became obvious that the Bf 110 was not capable of defending itself against RAF fighters, let alone escorting and protecting the bomber force, the *Jagdgruppen* were increasingly forced in to the close escort role. With their short range, it was a role for which they were ill suited. By September, the *Jagdgruppen* had by and large lost their freedom of action.

During the approximately four months of the Battle of Britain, from mid July to 31 October, the *Jagdflieger* lost 610 Bf 109Es and 235 Bf 110s while RAF fighter command lost 631 Hurricanes and 403 Spitfires. When the battered *Jagdgruppen* were withdrawn from operations on the Channel coast, neither side had won or lost. The *Jagdflieger,* created as a tactical force, fell short of winning anything of strategic importance during the Battle of Britain. This was not, however, due to any shortcoming on the part of the *Emil* or the pilots that mounted her.

Jerry Scutts points out that in fighter versus fighter combat results the Bf 109 came out the winner.

Fighter vs. Fighter Losses
219 Spitfires vs 180 Bf 109s
272 Hurricanes vs 153 Bf 109s

"491 Spitfires and Hurricanes against 333 Bf 109s lost was a ratio impressive enough to show just how effective the Luftwaffe's single seaters were."[*]

Toward the end of 1940, the *Luftwaffe* began pulling its *Jagdgruppen* from the Channel coast to be rested and refitted in Germany. JG 2 *Richthofen* and JG 26 *Schlageter* returned to the channel, the others did not. Hitler had turned his eyes eastward toward the 'real enemy', the Soviet Union.

* Luftwaffe Fighter Units, Europe 1939-41, Jerry Scutts, P. 38.

This Bf 109E-4 sitting in its revetment in France belongs to *Oberleutnant* **Heinz Ebeling,** *Staffelkapitän* **of 9/JG 26. The numeral 1 III.** *Gruppe* **bar are believed to be brown outlined in black.**

Very obviously carrying the 65/71/02 color scheme, a ground crewman adds Ebeling's 12th victory mark to his E-4. The young pilot was shot down over London on 5 November 1940 after having gained 18 victories.

Wearing his 'Mae West', colored flare bag, Very pistol and smoking his ever-present cigar, *Major* **Adolf Galland,** *Kommodore* of JG 26 *Schlageter,* climbs out of the cockpit of his E-4 after his 40th kill on 24 September. Galland claimed to have the only cigar lighter-equipped 109 in the *Luftwaffe.* (Bundesarchiv)

(Above Right) A ground crewman adds the 40th kill mark to the yellow rudder of Galland's machine. The control rod and horn just above the tail wheel are clearly visible. (Bundesarchiv)

Armored Windscreen

An E-4 of JG 1 with the supplementary armored windscreen. At the top of the photo, just above the pilot's head, can be seen the small knob used to push open the front part of the two-piece side glass, which appears to be open in this view. (Obert)

This French salvage crew is dismantling one of the results of the hard-fought Battle of Britain. Scenes like this were all too common as the *Jagdstaffeln* were slowly bled of their strength over England. Aircraft, of course, could be replaced much more easily than the hundreds of experienced fighter pilots that did not return. (Smithsonian)

(Above Left) When the Jagdstaffeln were restricted to close escort of the bombers, the shortness of the Bf 109's range became an even greater problem. On one mission alone, JG 26 lost 12 fighters when, "...after two hours flying time the bombers we were escorting had not yet reached the mainland on their return journey". Five [fighters] crashed on the shore and seven landed in the water.

While most of the Jagdstaffeln added additional darker camouflage to the sides of their aircraft, per regulations, 3/JG 1 chose to ignore the directive until well into 1941. (Obert)

Bf 109E-7, E-8 & E-9

During the late summer and early fall of 1940 small numbers of three other E variants began appearing.

The **E-7,** identical to the E-4 with the added capability of accepting fuselage racks for either a 300 liter drop tank or an ETC 50 or ETC 500 bomb rack. The spinner usually had a pointed tip rather than the MG FF cannon hole in it.

The **E-8** was an E-1 converted to carry a 300 liter drop tank.

The **E-9** was an E-7 converted to the reconnaissance role with an Rb 50/30 camera mounted in the fuselage and powered by a DB 601N engine.

The Balkans, Greece & Crete

During October, as the Battle of Britain was winding down to a stalemate, Mussolini, piqued at Hitler's military successes, decided to carve out some Roman destiny and began delivering ultimata to Greece. When these ultimata were rejected, the Italian Army launched an attack on Greece from Albania on 28 October 1940. After some initial successes, the Italian invasion was beaten back and after a hard winter of fighting almost half of Albania was in Greek hands. Fearing British involvement in the area, Hitler decided to come to the aid of his erstwhile ally by attacking Greece through Yugoslavia and Bulgaria after obtaining free passage through these countries. The Bf 109E equipped *Stab,* II and III/JG 27, I(*Jagd*)/LG 2 and II(*Schlacht*)/LG 2 began reaching bases in Rumania during March, followed by *Stab,* II and III/JG 77. Hitler's timetable, however, was upset when General Semovic overthrew the pro-Axis Yugoslav government and repudiated her treaties with Germany. On 25 March, Hitler ordered the destruction of Yugoslavia as well as the invasion of Greece.

On 6 April, the Wehrmacht, heavily supported by some 1200 aircraft struck, simultaneously attacking Yugoslavia and Greece. Only a handful of Yugoslav fighters managed to get into the air, most were destroyed on the ground. Ironically among those that did get airborne were the Bf 109Es of the Yugoslavian 6th Fighter Regiment. To avoid confusion the *Jagdgruppen* usually painted their cowls and rudders yellow. On 14 April, the Yugoslavs sued for peace.

Weather initially hampered air operations over Greece, where the small antiquated Greek fighter force was bolstered by one Blenheim, one Gladiator and two Hurricane squadrons. Air combat was fierce and bitter, if somewhat short, with little quarter given on either side. On the 13th, six Blenheims were bounced by Bf 109s and all were shot down. On the 23rd, when the remnants of the Greek Air Force and the RAF were evacuated to Crete, German losses stood at 164 against 72 for the British. Within a month, the *Jagdstaffeln* were in action supporting the airborne invasion of Crete. Opposition from Crete-based fighters was quickly subdued by the Bf 109Es of JG 77 supported by ZG 26. On 22 May, a lone Bf 109E-4/B of I/LG 2 attacked **HMS Fiji,** blowing a large hole in the cruiser's side. Thirty minutes later a second *Jabo* attacked, putting its 500 lb. bomb in the boiler room. **Fiji** capsized and went down. By 2 June, Crete was secure.

(Above Right) Hans Pichler of 7/JG 77 standing beside his Bf 109E-7 long range fighter. The underfuselage fuel tank rack was interchangeable with an ETC 50 or ETC 500 bomb rack, allowing the *Jagdstaffeln* to convert their machines to fighter bombers. This particular machine is an early E-7 and does not have the pointed spinner. (Obert)

Spinner Development

Bf 109E-4   **Bf 109E-7**

This E-7 fighter bomber, believed to be of JG 27, is equipped with an ETC 500 bomb rack. Not only have the nose and rudder been painted yellow but also the wing tips and a fuselage band have been painted. The yellow distemper has begun to chip and flake off the rudder. (Bundesarchiv)

Even under the severly primitive conditions that existed in the Balkans, the 'blackbirds' could quickly change an engine. (Obert)

Drop Tank

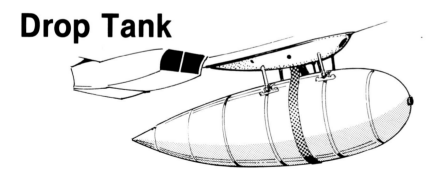

(Above Right) 'Black 10', a Bf 109E-3 of III/JG 77, was shot down while attacking an RAF aerodrome in Greece. It does not appear to carry the yellow nose usual to the Balkans Campaign. (IWM)

Bf 109E-4s of 7/JG 77 in Greece undergo preflight maintenance while the aircrew relax. (Obert)

Bf 109E/Trop

On 14 April 1941, 1./JG 27 arrived at Ain el Gazala Airfield in North Africa. While in transit to Sicily, where their aircraft had been tropicalized, JG 27 had briefly carried out missions in the Balkans. Tropicalization involved fitting a dust filter over the supercharger air intake and provision being made for emergency desert survival equipment including a carbine. Under the designation, **Bf 109E-4/Trop** and **E-5/Trop** the *Emils* of 1. *Staffel* JG 27 went into action on the 19th, engaging RAF No. 274 Squadron and claiming four Hurricanes for the loss of only one Bf 109E. Three days later, I/JG 27 was brought up to full three *Staffel* strength when 3/JG 27 arrived, going into battle almost immediately.

Mainly encountering Hurricanes, *Emil* acquitted herself well over the desert. Equipped with a fine airplane, the pilots were experienced, confident and ably led. Interestingly I/JG 27 carried, as the *Gruppe* emblem, a map of Africa superimposed on which was a spotted panther's head and a wide eyed Negro. The emblem had been carried since before the French Campaign and had no connection with the unit being posted to Africa, but was naturally thought to be a good omen for the personnel.

On 1 June, a fourth Bf 109E *Staffel* arrived in North Africa when 7/JG 26 transferred from Sicily to Gazala. Led by Oblt. Joachim Münchenberg, a Knight's Cross holder with 43 victories, its six E-7s were a welcome reinforcement.

In mid-June, accompanied by heavy air fighting, British forces launched Operation 'Battleaxe' to relieve Tobruk. Quickly blunting the British attack, Rommel launched a counterattack on the 17th. "After the failure of 'Battleaxe', both sides settled down to a period of recoupment and a race to build up supplies before the next offensive began." Hitler, however, was looking eastward and building up men and material preparing for the invasion of Russia. Rommel's supplies were meager. It was not until September that additional fighter reinforcements arrived. On 14 September II/JG 27, which had been pulled out of the Russian Campaign to re-equip with the new Bf 109F, arrived in Africa.

With the arrival of the 109F, *Emil's* first-line fighter days were numbered. The E-series were, however, still in use as fighter-bombers and reconnaissance fighters until well into 1942.

(Above Right) Immediately upon its arrival, I/JG 27 began flying missions. Still in its European paint scheme, this Bf 109E-4/Trop, flown by the *Gruppen Adjujtant Oblt*. Ludwig Franzisket, is escorting a Ju 87 of II/St.G 2 on its return flight from the Tobruk area. (Bundesarchiv)

Sand Filter

Closed

Open

The reason for the sandfilter!

Oberfähnrich (Ensign) Hans-Joachim Marsielle, the 'black sheep' of the *Luftwaffe* arrived in Africa with seven kills to his credit. Marseille, wearing the summer flying helmet, is in a machine still carrying a yellow nose and the standard European paint scheme. Marseille also is wearing a summer weight European dark blue tunic. (Bundesarchiv)

(Above Right) A well known *Rotte*, 'White 3' and '8' of 1/JG 27 on patrol over the Western Desert. '8' carries a much thicker fuselage band than '3'. (Bundesarchiv)

Wearing a mixture of European and African clothing, these pilots of I/JG 27 are briefed in front of their Bf 109E-4/Trops, which carry a mixture of European and African paint schemes. The first, second and fourth aircraft are camouflaged in the standard European grey scheme with yellow noses while the third machine has its upper surfaces painted in the African scheme of Sand Yellow (79), Olive Green (80) and Light Blue (78). To each aircraft has been added the Mediterranean theater white fuselage band. (Smithsonian)

The Bf 109E-7s of 7/JG 26 carried *Oblt.* Müchenberg's red heart emblem on both sides of their yellow noses. All machines were in the standard European grays and each carried *Schlageter's* script 'S' on a white shield on the port side. (Smithsonian)

By November 1941, 10/JG 27, the *Jabo Staffel* of JG 27, had moved into the Mediterranean area still carrying their European scheme with yellow noses and rudders, only the addition of a white band indicates the Mediterranean theater. (Smithsonian)

This ETC 500 rack carries the warning "remove cover before removing rack". The single word toward the front of the rack translates "lock". The inscription on the bomb reads, "Nothing left but a cloud of dust". This view offers an excellent view of the bomb attachment pins. (Bundesarchiv)

With the arrival of the Bf 109F, the *Emil* series was quickly relegated to the *Jabo* and reconnaissance role. This E-7/Trop, possibly of 10(*Jabo*)/JG 27 carries a white half-band around the lower cowling. (Bundesarchiv)

Barbarossa

Although the *Jagdflieger* had been converting to the **Bf 109F** series as quickly as possible, over a third of the 440 Bf 109 fighters committed to the opening attack against Russia were *Emils*. Bf 109Es equipped II/ and III/JG 27 in the central sector, I/ and II/JG 52, II/ and III/JG 77 and I(*Jagd*)/LG 2 in the southern sector, and II/JG 54 in the northern sector. While somewhat dated by Luftwaffe standards, the Bf 109E was certainly ". . .more than adequate to deal with the vast majority of Soviet aircraft it would meet initially — particularly when in the hands of the very high quality pilots which most of the *Jagdflieger* were." Worthy of note is the fact that in the 1940 campaign against France and the Low Countries, the *Jagdflieger* was able to commit over 1000 Bf 109 fighters, however in 1941 with fighters diverted along the Channel coast, in the Balkans and Greece, in Norway and North Africa, less than 500 were available for the opening phases of 'Barbarossa' the greatest military campaign in recorded history. One wonders what would be written on the pages of history, had the German war machine been able to concentrate its total forces on what Hitler called "the natural enemy".

At early dawn on 22 June 1941, the *Luftwaffe* launched a pre-emptive strike with 637 bombers and 231 fighters on the 31 known Russian airfields. Surprise was complete, hundreds of Russian aircraft were destroyed, with only two German aircraft failing to return. The attacks continued all day and by nightfall, almost 300 Russian aircraft had been claimed by fighters in aerial combat and at least 800 more had been destroyed on the ground. Most historians agree that Russian losses were at least 1200 aircraft on the first day and some estimates have ranged as high as 1800. The *Luftwaffe* lost just 35 machines. One of those lost, however, was Major Schellmann, *Kommodore* of JG 27. Flying a Bf 109E, Schellmann shot down an I-16 raising his score to 25 (12 in Spain), when his aircraft was crippled by debris from the Russian fighter. Forced to bail out over Russian territory, Schellmann was captured and shot by the NKVD two days later. Little quarter would be given or sought in the East by either side.

By 29 June, after one week of fighting, *OKW* reported the destruction of at least 4,017 Soviet aircraft for the loss of 150. After only ten days at the front, II/JG 27 was pulled out and sent back to Germany to be re-equipped with Bf 109Fs. By August, II/JG 52 had, in the main, been re-equipped with Bf 109Fs, although they continued to operate a few *Emils* well into the winter.

As production tempo of the Bf 109F increased and battlefield attrition took its toll of *Emils,* the fall of 1941 saw Bf 109Es rapidly disappear from first-line fighter strength reports along the Eastern Front. By early spring 1942, few *Emils* could be found operating in Russia in the purely fighter role. Some Bf 109E fighter-bombers were to equip the *Jabo Staffeln* well into 1942 and, in the north, JG 5 was formed on Bf 109Es during early 1942.

(Above Right) 'White 3' of III/JG 54, a Bf 109E-4 with cockpit armor, during the earlier stages of *Barbarossa*. The yellow rudder and rear fuselage band are Eastern Front markings (yellow wingtips came later). The yellow nose is a carry over from previous campaigns.

Early in the Russian Campaign, 8/JG 54 was still flying a few Bf 109E-3s into battle. This machine, carrying high Light Blue sides and a yellow nose, would look less out of place in the early stages of the Battle of Britain. The experts all claim this nose to be yellow rather than a dark color, pointing out that on certain types of film used during the '40s, yellow appeared very dark. Just the same, it sure looks very similar to a blackgreen nose.

While the *Luftwaffe* had quickly gained control of the air by smashing the Red Air Force almost overnight, fierce resistance was encountered from ground fire.

(Below Left) By the time the early winter of 1941 had set in, most of the Bf 109Es had converted to the *Jabo* or fighter-bomber role. This Bf 109E-3/B is equipped with the added windscreen armor.

Regardless of temperature, conditions or circumstances, maintenance had to be performed. Fortunately this appears to be a relatively sunny and warm day for winter in the East.

Don't Forget...

...the other half of this GREAT Two Part Set!